NEW POWER PLANT

GAURAV SINGH PATEL

Pollution

Contents

Contents

Preface

If we look around us today, we find that today almost all our needs are based on electricity and we are making new efforts every day to make that electricity. And in this effort, we are fulfilling our wishes very well, but we are harming our environment in the same amount. Today we are getting 70 % of our total quantity of electricity from coal power plants only. But by getting electricity in this way, many harmful gases like oxides of nitrogen and sulfur dioxide, oxides of carbon are coming out in abundance in the environment, which can emerge as a serious problem in future, so now we have to use this exhaust of electricity generation. Will also have to stop a new power plant will have to be designed. As a result, in this proposal, we have proposed a new power plant which is more efficient than the existing power plant, as well as the exhaust which we produce; we can also use it.

ONE
FIRST PROPOSAL

DRY ICE ACETYLENE

POWER PLANT

(DIA POWER PLANT)

TWO

Main Problem

As we all know that in today's time of modernity, energy plays an important role, somewhere today we are getting almost every need of our energy in the form of electricity. And with this, today we generate 77% of electricity from coal power plants in India. According to the report of the Ministry of New and Renewable Energy, gross electricity consumption in 2019 was 1208 kWh per capita. From this data, we understand one thing that distribution of so much electricity in such a large population is a challenging task. Keep the production of your electricity in such a way that it is efficient in cost and does not harm the environment; whereas in today's time we do not get to see this, the environment is being polluted in the production of electricity, then in this paper proposal After reaching the root of this problem, we have proposed a new power plant, which is named Dry Ice Acetylene Power Plant (DIA Power

Plant).

Power plant, Dry Ice Acetylene power plant, Acetylene power plant, DIA power plant, Multi purpose power plant, Most Efficient Power plant.

THREE

PROBLEM OF MODERN POWER PLANT

According to the report of Economic Times, the power received through different means and their percentage in the power generation capacity in India are as follows.

Sources	Share (MW)	Percentage
Thermal	2,21,803	64%
Renewable	70,648	21%
Hydro	45,487	13%
Gas	24,867	7.21%
Nuclear	6780	2%
diesel	838	0.24%

As we have seen above, in India, 64% of the power generation source is thermal and in thermal power generation we use coal. When coal burns, we give the energy obtained from it to the boiler, in which the water is converted into steam; and later this steam spins the turbine, which generates power.

But there is a serious problem here, which is often ignored today; but we cannot leave the future on this situation. The problem arises when we look at exhaust produced by burning coal. Let's take a look at pulses once on the exhaust caused by burning coal –

Exhaust Gases	Percentage
N_2	72-77 %
CO_2	12-14 %
H_2O	8-10 %
O_2	3-5 %

After studying this chart, 2 problems arise in front of us.

FOUR

PROBLEM 1

According to the report of Economic Times, the power received through different means and their percentage in the power generation capacity in India are as follows.

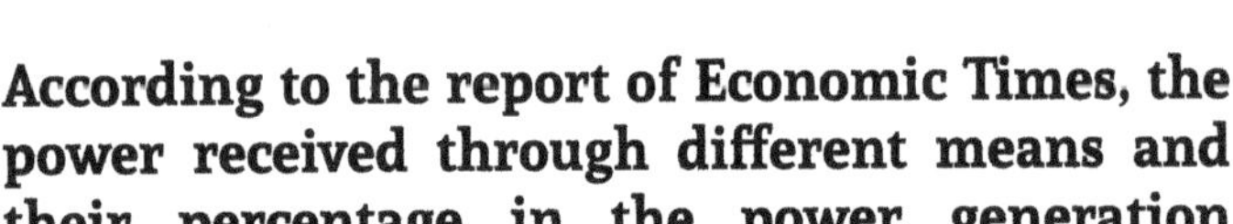

As we are seeing that by burning coal, the highest amount of N2 gas and then CO2 is produced, which has very harmful effects on the environment and humans.

Nitrogen effect-

- If we see deeply, then we will find that nitrogen is safe to breathe only when mixed with the appropriate amount of oxygen.
- Excess nitrogen in the atmosphere can produce pollutants such as ammonia and ozone, which

can impair our ability to breathe, limit visibility and alter plant growth. When excess nitrogen comes back to Earth from the atmosphere. It can harm the health of forests, soils and water ways.

carbon dioxide effect-

- They cause climate change by trapping heat, and they also contribute to respiratory diseases from smog and air pollution.
- Exposure to CO2 can produce a variety of health effects. They may include headaches, dizziness, restlessness, a tingling or pain or needles, feeling, difficulty breathing, sweating, tiredness, increased heart rate, elevated blood pressure, coma, asphyxia and convulsions.

NOx effect-

- High levels of NOx can have a negative effect on vegetation by making it more susceptible to disease and frost damage.
- NOx gas has adverse effects on the ozone layer in the troposphere area of the earth's atmosphere, which results in the green house effects and global warming.

The poison that we are leaving in our society today, we have to stop it somewhere for the future.

FIVE

PROBLEM 2

After pollution and health loss, another problem that comes to our notice is that coal is being used only to provide heat to the boiler. The exhaust generated by it is not being used.

Actually, we cannot even use the exhaust obtained from coal because it contains a mixture of many gases like nitrogen, carbon dioxide etc. and to make it useful, the gases will have to be separated first, which will not be a profitable industry idea for us. So our final problem is, how can we use that exhaust in our own way.1.4 proposal

Our main task is to deliver heat to the boiler by any means; and from that heat the water turns into steam, and that steam spins the turbine to generate power. But it is not necessary that all

the time we provide heat to the boiler by burning coal, now the time has come that in some way we should use some other fuel instead of coal which does not spread much pollution in the environment and with its energy. Along with this, we can also make full use of its exhaust.

We will use acetylene in place of time in our paper proposal and will also produce it in our plant and will also produce exhaust complete carbon dioxide after burning it and supply the product made from it in the market; in this way the environment will be completely safe.

SIX

OUR SOLUTION ACETYLENE GAS

Acetylene also called ethyne, is the simplest and best known member of the hydrocarbon series, containing one or more pairs of carbon atoms linked by triple bonds [C2 H2] called the acetylenic series, or alkynes. It is a colorless inflammable gas widely used as a fuel in oxyacetylene welding and cutting of metals and as raw materials in the synthesis of many organic chemicals and plastics.

- Density – 1.17729 g/l = 1.1772 kg/m^3(at 0°c, 101.3 kPa)

-

Melting point – -80.8°c (-113.4°F, 192.3 K) Triple point at 1.27 atm

•

Sublimation – -84°c, -119°F, 189 K (1 atm)

•

Vapor pressure – 44.2 atm (20°c)

•

Combustion heat – 48.2 MJ/kg

CaC_2 (g) + $2H_2O$ (l) ---------------- C_2H_2 (g) + $Ca(OH)_2$ (aq.) [Production of acetylene gas]

$2C_2H_2$ (g) + 5 O_2 (g) ---------------- $4CO_2$ (g) + 2 H_2O (g) [Burning of acetylene gas]

or C_2H_2 (g) + 5/2 O_2 (g) ----------------- $2CO_2$ (g) + H_2O (g)

SEVEN

WORKING OF POWER PLANT

The entire process of generating electricity and making full use of the exhaust is completed in 10 steps in this DIA power plant. In the first step, we purify the water and store it. In the second stage store, we produce acetylene gas by mixing calcium carbide with pure water. In the third step, by burning acetylene, the generated heat is sent to the boiler, due to which the water is converted into steam. In the fourth stage, steam is sent to the turbine, due to which the turbine starts rotating. In the fifth stage, the turbine is connected to the generator, which generates electricity.

Now we turn our attention back to the exhaust and in the sixth step, carbon dioxide is purified from the exhaust. Generally, only carbon dioxide is obtained in the combustion of acetylene. But sometimes carbon monoxide is

formed along with carbon dioxide in low combustion, which is harmful; it is very necessary for us to separate it. After purifying, in the next seventh stage, the carbon dioxide gas is sent to the compressor, after that the compressed carbon dioxide is sent to the condenser in the next eighth stage and the condensed gas is passed through the expansion valve in the next ninth stage, after that in the next final stage Dry ice is separated by separator.

PRECAUTION

Incomplete combustion of acetylene produces carbon monoxide [CO] gas, which acts as a poison, and if we do not have complete combustion at all, then we can skip our truncated phase which will increase the cast efficiency further.

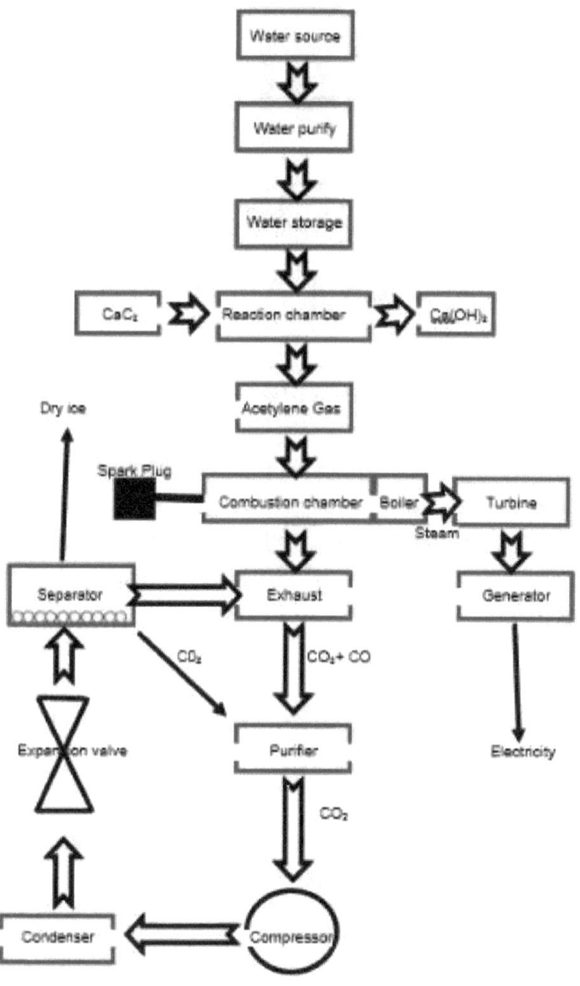
Water source
Water purify
Water storage
CaC_2
Reaction chamber
$Ca(OH)_2$
Acetylene Gas
Dry ice
Spark Plug
Combustion chamber
Boiler
Turbine
Steam
Separator
Exhaust
Generator
CO_2
CO_2+ CO
Purifier
Electricity
CO_2
Condenser
Compressor

EIGHT

COST ESTIMATION

Before designing a power plant, we need to know whether the new design we have made is cost efficient or not. In cost estimation we will compare this power plant with thermal power plant.

Dry ice acetylene power plant (DIA power plant)

In this new proposal we are using acetylene gas in place of time and converting exhaust into dry ice.

Combustion heat of acetylene = 48.2 MJ/kg

Mean per kg acetylene gas can generate 48.2 MJ energy after combustion. Now we will calculate

how much we have to pay for generate 1 kg acetylene.

CaC_2 (g) + $2H_2O$ (l) -------------- C_2H_2 (g) + $Ca(OH)_2$ (aq.) [biproduct]

For generation of 1 mole acetylene we have to need 1 mole calcium carbonate and 2 mole water.

Mass of 1 mole C_2H_2 = 26.03708 gram

Mass of 1 mole CaC_2 = 64.0994 gram

For generation of 26.036708 gram C2H2 we have to required 64.0994 gram of calcium carbide. So to get 1 kg of acetylene, we will need 2.461850 kg of calcium carbide. And according to exportsindia.com and Madhuraj Industrial Gases Pvt Ltd,

the price of calcium carbide is 11000 - 12500 / metric ton.

So feet say calcium carbide price = 11-12.5 Rs

On taking the middle = 11.75 Rs

Factor of Safety = 2.0

Final foot kg calcium carbide price = 23.5 Rs

Therefore, to produce one kilogram of acetylene, we will have to invest 57.853475 Rs, from which we will get 48.2 MJ of energy and we will get two new products which we can sell in the right market and make our power plant profitable.

calcium hydroxide

CaC_2 (g) + $2H_2O$ (l)---------------- C_2H_2 (g) + $Ca(OH)_2$ (aq.)

From 1 kg of calcium carbide, 1.155915 kg of calcium hydroxide is produced. Therefore, 2.461850 kg of calcium carbide will be required to produce 1 kg of acetylene and 2.845689 kg of calcium hydroxide will be produced.

And according to today's market, calcium hydroxide is sold at Rs 7.5/kg, so in producing 1

kg of acetylene, we will make calcium hydroxide byproduct worth 21.3426675.

Exhaust carbon dioxide

We will convert the exhaust carbon dioxide again into dry ice by rotating it in a cycle.

$2C_2H_2$ (g) + 5 O_2 (g)-------------- $4CO_2$ (g) + 2 H_2O (g)

So, on complete combustion of 1 kg of acetylene, we will get 3.3801 kg of carbon dioxide, which goes on to be converted into dry ice.

Factor of Safety = 1.7

So out of 3.3801 kg of carbon dioxide, only 1.98,892 kg of carbon dioxide was converted into dry ice and the minimum price of dry ice according to today's market is Rs.45/kg. So after burning one kilogram of acetylene, we will get dry ice worth Rs.89.472.

Total revenue with carbon dioxide and calcium hydroxide

For per kg acetylene gas

Total revenue = revenue with calcium hydroxide + revenue with carbon dioxide

= 21.342667 Rs + 89.472 Rs

= 110.814 Rs

NINE

Thermal Power Plant

Bituminous coal, subbituminous coal or lignite coal are used in thermal power plants

Coal	Calorific value
Bituminous	24 MJ/Kg
Subbituminous	22 MJ/Kg
lignite	17 MJ/Kg

Average calorific value = 21 MJ/kg

Acetylene calorific value = 48.2 MJ/kg (with 1.4 factor of safety)

Therefore, we have to burn 2.295 times (2.295 kg) of coal to get as much energy as 1 kg of acetylene, which costs 10 rupees per kg in today's market, in which 20% carbon is present.

In the end, we have to invest Rs 22.95 to get the energy from as much as 1 kg of acetylene. While 57.85 rupees have to be invested in acetylene to get the same energy, yet our DIA power plant is more efficient than thermal power plant, let's see it further.

TEN

Exhaust Utilization Process

The exhaust utilization process is completed in 5 steps; in the first step, a small amount of carbon monoxide mixed with carbon dioxide is passed through a high pressure water container, which separates carbon dioxide and carbon monoxide. From here we take CO formed in an economiser, in which CO reacts with oxygen to generate carbon dioxide gas and energy.

$2CO(g) + O_2(g)$ -------------- $2CO_2(g)$ + Energy

After this, the carbon dioxide gas is taken again into the high pressure water container. After

this, in the second stage, we send the received carbon dioxide to the compressor, and in the third stage we send the compressed gas to the condenser; after that in the fourth stage we send the condensed gas to the expansion valve, after which the carbon dioxide starts converting into dry ice. After that, in the final stage, the dry ice is separated in the separator and the carbon dioxide, which could not be converted into dry ice, is sent back to the compressor for recycling.

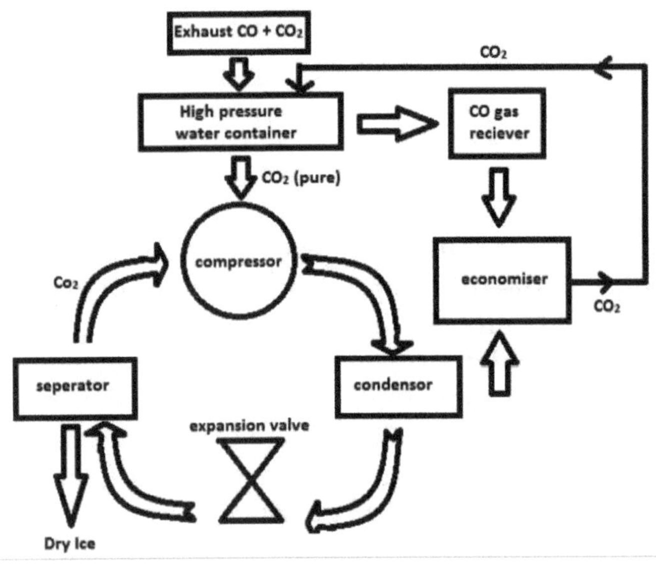

Manufacturing of solid carbon dioxide or dry ice pressure – enthalpy diagram

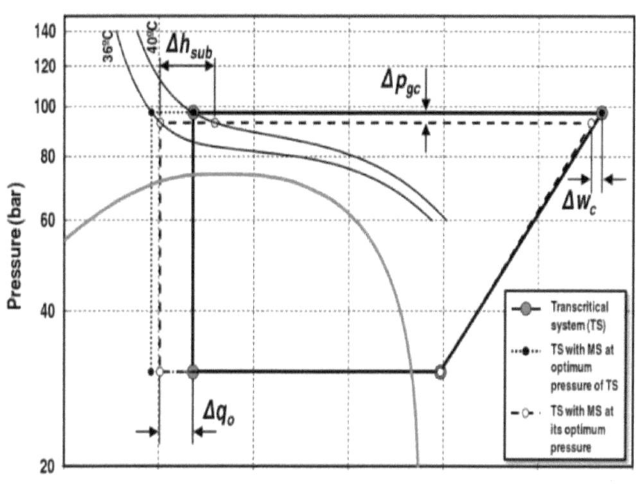

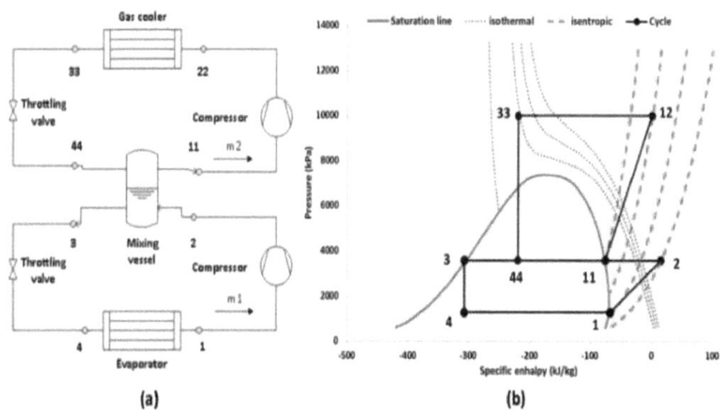

thermodynamic property of CO_2

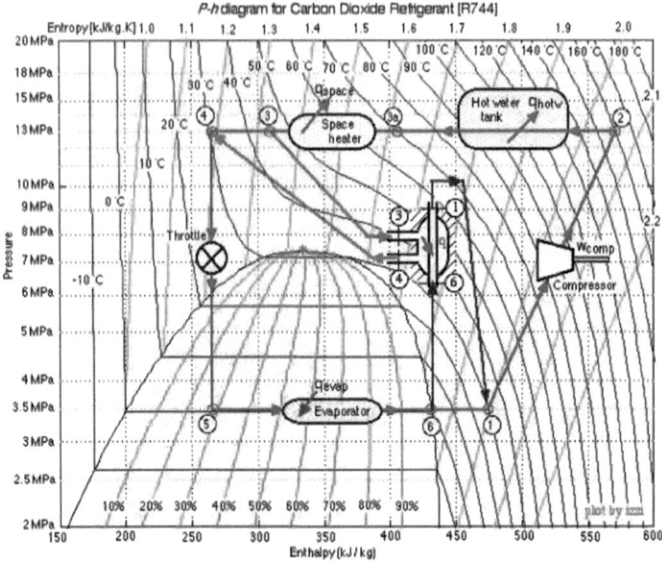
P-h diagram for Carbon Dioxide Refrigerant [R744]
Entropy [kJ/kg.K]
Pressure
Enthalpy [kJ / kg]
Space heater
Hot water tank
Throttle
Evaporator
Compressor
plot by zzn

ELEVEN

RESULT

Therefore, in this way, by replacing coal in power generation, the advantage of acetylene gas is that there is not much gas mixture in the exhaust that comes out in it, so we can use those gases also. We also make acetylene gas through calcium carbide, and purified water. In this process we get biproduct calcium hydroxide, for which the market doors are open.

Therefore, through this type of power plant, we can not only generate power but also save our environment from harmful gases. And if the products generated by the power plant like calcium hydroxide and dry ice are properly transported to the right market, then we will find this multipurpose power plant more economical than the old power plant.

TWELVE
CONCLUSION

Full Project chart

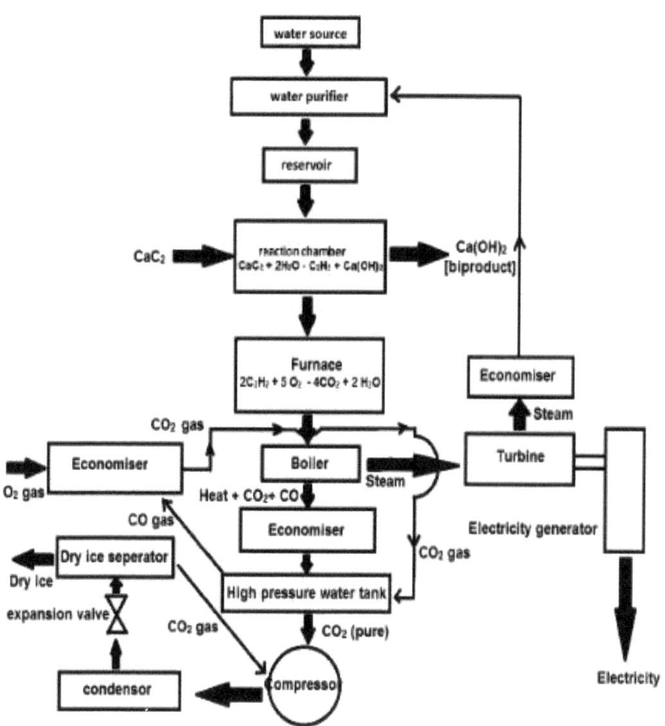

Comparative Study of Thermal Power Plant and Dry Key Power Plant (DIA Power Plant) on the basis of Result obtained -

Here we will compare coal and acetylene by assuming that the energy obtained from them (MJ / kg) will be equal.

Fuel type	Gain Energy	Fuel required/Kg	Cost of Fuel	Biproducts name	Biproducts in Kg	Biproducts price	Total	Pollution
Coal	48.2 MJ	2.295 Kg	22.95 Rs	-	-	-	-22.95Rs	CO_2,NO_x
Acetylene	48.2 MJ	1 Kg	57.85 Rs	$Ca(OH)_2$	2.46 Kg	23.45 Rs	+55.07Rs	-
				Dry Ice	1.98 Kg	89.472 Rs		

So we can clearly see where we are getting only energy in thermal power plants; on the other hand, we get the same amount of energy in dry acetylene power plants as well as 95.19% return as its biproduct. And almost our entire power plant will run free of cost. Also, we will not harm our environment in the form of pollution.

THIRTEEN

REFERENCES

[1] Thermodynamic Properties of R744 (Carbon Dioxide - CO2) Engineering Thermodynamics by Israel Urieli.

[2] A comparative study of CO2 refrigeration systems by Evangelos Bellos Christos Tzivanidis

[3] Czapla, Nicholas & Inamdar, Harshad & Barta, Riley & Groll, Eckhard. (2016). Theoretical Analysis of the Impact of an Energy Recovery Expansion Device in a CO 2 Refrigeration System.

[4] Wang, Zhifang & Zheng, Danxing & Jin, Hongguang. (2009). Energy integration of acetylene and power polygeneration by flowrate-exergy diagram. Applied Energy. 86. 372-379. 10.1016/j.apenergy.2008.05.011.

[5] Anand, M. & Devi, G. & Srinivasan, Gokul & Prakasha, G S & Thangavelu, Lakshmanan. (2021). A critical study on acetylene as an alternative fuel for transportation. AIP Conference Proceedings. 2396. 020005. 10.1063/5.0066773.

FOURTEEN
SECOND PROPOSAL

ELECTROCHEMICAL ACETYLENE POWER PLANT

(ECA POWER PLANT)

FIFTEEN

Main problem

If we look around us today, we find that today almost all our needs are based on electricity and we are making new efforts every day to make that electricity. And in this effort, we are fulfilling our wishes very well, but we are harming our environment in the same amount. Today we are getting 70 % of our total quantity of electricity from coal power plants only. But by getting electricity in this way, many harmful gases like oxides of nitrogen and sulfur dioxide, oxides of carbon are coming out in abundance in the environment, which can emerge as a serious problem in future, so now we have to use this exhaust of electricity generation. Will also have to stop a new power plant will have to be designed. As a result, in this proposal, we have proposed a new power plant which is more efficient than the existing power plant, as well as the exhaust which we produce; we can also use it.

SIXTEEN

DOWNSIDE OF RECENT POWER STATION

According to the report of Economic Times, the facility received through totally different suggests that and their proportion within the power generation capability in Bharat area unit as follows.

Sources	Share (MW)	Percentage
Thermal	2,21,803	64%
Renewable	70,648	21%
Hydro	45,487	13%
Gas	24,867	7.21%
Nuclear	6780	2%
diesel	838	0.24%

As we've seen on top of that, in India, sixty fourths of the ability generation supply is thermal and in thermal power generation we have a tendency to use coal. Once coal burns, we have a tendency to provide the energy obtained from it to the boiler, within which the water is reborn into steam;, and later this steam spins the rotary engine, which generates power.
But there's a significant drawback here, one that is usually unheeded today; however, we have a tendency to not leave the long run on this case. The matter arises once we check out exhaust made by burning coal. Let's take a glance at pulses once on the exhaust caused by burning coal –

Exhaust Gases	Percentage
N_2	72-77 %
CO_2	12-14 %
H_2O	8-10 %
O_2	3-5 %

After studying this chart, 2 problems arise in front of us.

SEVENTEEN

PROBLEM 1

As we are seeing that by burning coal, the highest amount of N_2 gas and then CO_2 is produced, which has very harmful effects on the environment and humans.

Nitrogen effect-

• If we see deeply, then we will find that nitrogen is safe to breathe only when mixed with the appropriate amount of oxygen.

• Excess nitrogen in the atmosphere can produce pollutants such as ammonia and ozone, which can impair our ability to breathe, limit visibility and alter plant growth. When excess nitrogen comes back to Earth from the atmosphere. It can harm the health of forests, soils and water ways.

carbon dioxide effect-

• They cause climate change by trapping heat, and they also contribute to respiratory diseases from smog and air pollution.

• Exposure to CO2 can produce a variety of health effects. They may include headaches, dizziness, restlessness, a tingling or pain or needles, feeling, difficulty breathing, sweating, tiredness, increased heart rate, elevated blood pressure, coma, asphyxia and convulsions.

NOx effect-

• High levels of NOx can have a negative effect on vegetation by making it more susceptible to disease and frost damage.

• NOx gas has adverse effects on the ozone layer in the troposphere area of the earth's atmosphere, which results in the green house effects and global warming.

The poison that we are leaving in our society today, we have to stop it somewhere for the future.

EIGHTEEN

PROBLEM 2

After pollution and health loss, another problem that comes to our notice is that coal is being used only to provide heat to the boiler. The exhaust generated by it is not being used.

Actually, we cannot even use the exhaust obtained from coal because it contains a mixture of many gases like nitrogen, carbon dioxide etc. and to make it useful, the gases will have to be separated first, which will not be a profitable industry idea for us. So our final problem is, how can we use that exhaust in our own way.

NINETEEN

PROPOSAL

Our main task is to deliver heat to the boiler by any means; and from that heat the water turns into steam, and that steam spins the turbine to generate power. But it is not necessary that all the time we provide heat to the boiler by burning coal, now the time has come that in some way we should use some other fuel instead of coal which does not spread much pollution in the environment and with its energy. Along with this, we can also make full use of its exhaust.

We will use acetylene in place of time in our paper proposal and will also produce it in our plant and will also produce exhaust complete carbon dioxide after burning it and supply the product made from it in the market; in this way the environment will be completely safe.

TWENTY

About Acetylene Gas

Acetylene also called ethyne, is the simplest and best known member of the hydrocarbon series, containing one or more pairs of carbon atoms linked by triple bonds [C2 H2] called the acetylenic series, or alkynes. It is a colorless inflammable gas widely used as a fuel in oxyacetylene welding and cutting of metals and as raw materials in the synthesis of many organic chemicals and plastics.

- Density – 1.17729 g/l = 1.1772 kg/m^3(at 0°c, 101.3 kPa)
-

Melting point – -80.8°c (-113.4°F, 192.3 K) Triple point at 1.27 atm

- **Sublimation – -84°c, -119°F, 189 K (1 atm)**

- **Vapor pressure – 44.2 atm (20°c)**

- **Combustion heat – 48.2 MJ/kg**

CaC_2 (g) + $2H_2O$ (l) ---------------- C_2H_2 (g) + $Ca(OH)_2$ (aq.) [Production of acetylene gas]

$2C_2H_2$ (g) + 5 O_2 (g) ---------------- $4CO_2$ (g) + 2 H_2O (g) [Burning of acetylene gas]

or C_2H_2 (g) + 5/2 O_2 (g) ----------------- $2CO_2$ (g) + H_2O (g)

TWENTY-ONE

WORKING BLOCK DIAGRAM

The entire process of generating electricity and making full use of the exhaust is completed in 7 steps in this DIA power plant. In the first step, we purify the water and store it. In the second stage store, we produce acetylene gas by mixing calcium carbide with pure water. In the third step, by burning acetylene, the generated heat is sent to the boiler, due to which the water is converted into steam. In the fourth stage, steam is sent to the turbine, due to which the turbine starts rotating. In the fifth stage, the turbine is connected to the generator, which generates electricity.

Now we turn our attention back to the exhaust and in the sixth step, carbon dioxide is purified from the exhaust. Generally, only carbon dioxide is obtained in the combustion of acetylene. But sometimes carbon monoxide is

formed along with carbon dioxide in low combustion, which is harmful; it is very necessary for us to separate it. After purifying, in the next seventh stage, the carbon dioxide gas is sent to the electrochemical battery, and that electrochemical battery converts CO_2 into electricity and hydrogen gas. From here we can use electricity separately and separate our H_2 gas as a fuel.

Precautions

Incomplete combustion of acetylene produces carbon monoxide [CO] gas, which acts as a poison, and if we do not have complete combustion at all, then we can skip our truncated phase which will increase the cast efficiency further.

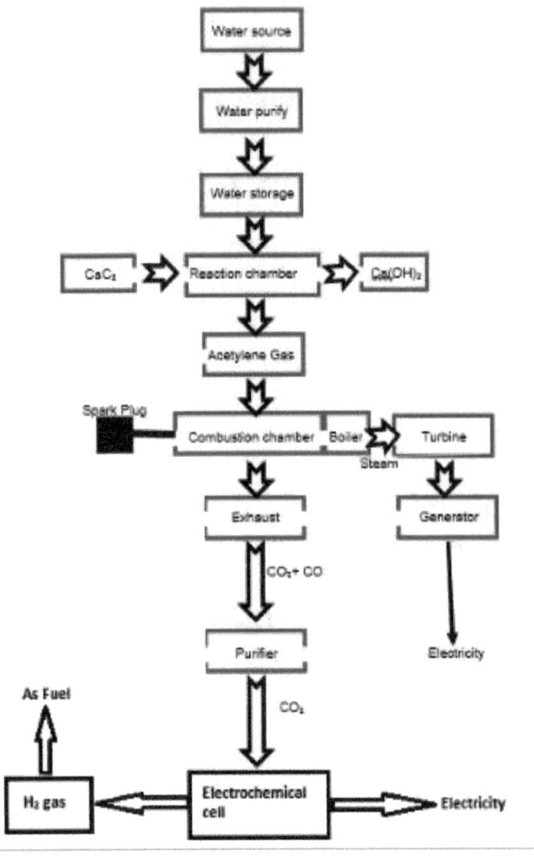
Water source
Water purify
Water storage
CaC_2
Reaction chamber
$Ca(OH)_2$
Acetylene Gas
Spark Plug
Combustion chamber
Boiler
Steam
Turbine
Exhaust
Generator
CO_2 + CO
Purifier
Electricity
As Fuel
CO_2
H_2 gas
Electrochemical cell
Electricity

TWENTY-TWO

About Hydrogen gas

Hydrogen is easily the most abundant element in the universe. It is found in the sun and most of the stars, and the planet Jupiter is composed mostly of hydrogen.On Earth, hydrogen is found in the greatest quantities as water. It is present as a gas in the atmosphere only in tiny amounts – less than 1 part per million by volume. Any hydrogen that does enter the atmosphere quickly escapes the Earth's gravity into outer space.Most hydrogen is produced by heating natural gas with steam to form syngas (a mixture of hydrogen and carbon monoxide). The syngas is separated to give hydrogen. Hydrogen can also be produced by the electrolysis of water.

Hydrogen is an essential element for life. It is present in water and in almost all the molecules in living things. However, hydrogen itself does not play a particularly active role. It remains bonded to carbon and oxygen atoms, while the chemistry of life takes place at the more active sites involving, for example, oxygen, nitrogen and phosphorus.

- Density – 0.08375 kg/m^3
- Melting point – -259.2 °C
- Vapor pressure –

Temperature(°C)	Vapor Pressure (mmHg)	Vapor Pressure (kPa)
0	4.6	0.61
5	6.5	0.87
10	9.2	1.23
15	12.8	1.71
20	17.5	2.33

- Combustion heat – 120-142 MJ/kg

	Various Fuels	Heat value
1	Hydrogen (H_2)	120-142 MJ/kg
2	Methane (CH_4)	50-55 MJ/kg
3	Methanol (CH_3OH)	22.7 MJ/kg
4	Dimethyl ether - DME (CH_3OCH_3)	29 MJ/kg
5	Petrol/gasoline	44-46 MJ/kg
6	Diesel fuel	42-46 MJ/kg
7	Crude oil	42-47 MJ/kg
8	Liquefied petroleum gas (LPG)	46-51 MJ/kg
9	Natural gas	42-55 MJ/kg
10	Hard black coal (IEA definition)	>23.9 MJ/kg
11	Hard black coal (Australia & Canada)	c. 25 MJ/kg
12	Sub-bituminous coal (IEA definition)	17.4-23.9 MJ/kg
13	Sub-bituminous coal (Australia & Canada)	c. 18 MJ/kg
14	Lignite/brown coal (IEA definition)	<17.4 MJ/kg
15	Lignite/brown coal (Australia, electricity)	c. 10 MJ/kg
16	Firewood (dry)	16 MJ/kg
17	Natural uranium, in LWR (normal reactor)	500 GJ/kg
18	Natural uranium, in LWR with U & Pu recycle	650 GJ/kg
19	Natural uranium, in FNR	28,000 GJ/kg
20	Uranium enriched to 3.5%, in LWR	3900 GJ/kg

TWENTY-THREE

ELECTROCHEMICAL CELL

A schematic example of the proposed hybrid Na-CO_2 mobileular is provided in Figure 1. The virtual photos of the gadget also are provided in Figure S1. This gadget should paintings constantly with Na steel and CO_2 as gasoline on the anode and feedstock fueloline on the cathode, respectively. Na is appeared as a promising candidate alternatively for Li in phrases of its electrochemically comparable conduct along side low cost (30 instances inexpensive than Li) from herbal abundance and environmental friendliness (Noorden, 2014; Kwak et al., 2015). The Na steel anode is saved in an natural electrolyte to save you an immediate corrosion from an aqueous electrolyte isolating via way of means of Na incredible ionic conductor (NASICON) membrane. The standard response mechanisms are composed of a

chemical response and an electrochemical response

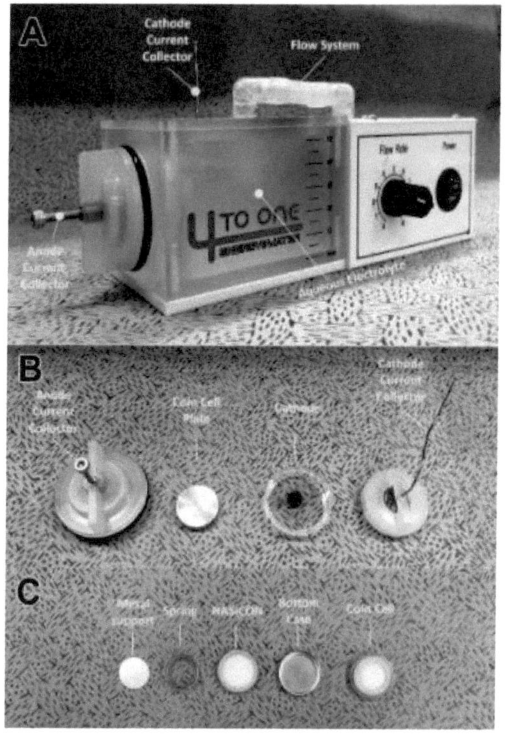

Hybrid Na-CO_2 Cell

$CO_2(aq) + H_2O(l)$ ------------- $H_2CO_3(aq)$ (equation1)

$H_2CO_3(aq)$ ---------------- HCO^{3-} (aq) + H^+ (aq) (equation2)

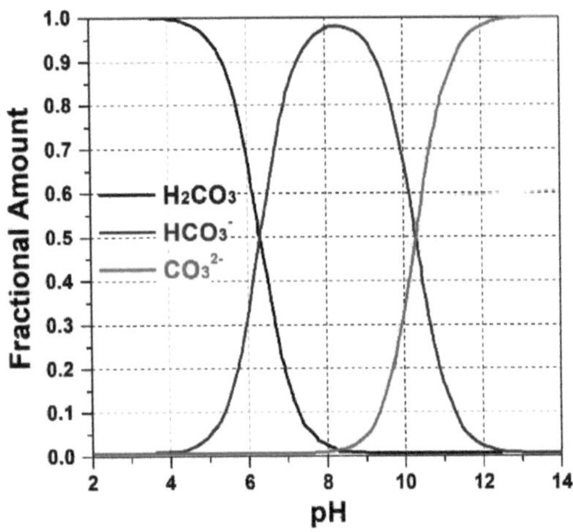

When CO_2 is purged into an aqueous answer (e.g., distilled water, seawater, NaOH answer), CO_2 dissolution proceeds and carbonic acid ($H_2CO_3(aq)$) is fashioned via the hydration of CO_2 (Equation 1). For a standard

country circumstance in natural water, this spontaneous chemical equilibrium of CO_2 hydration is decided through the hydration equilibrium consistent (Kh = 1.70 three 10-three) (Housecroft and Sharpe, 2005). Then, the carbonic acid dissociates into HCO3- and H+ decided through the primary acid dissociation consistent (Ka1 = 4.forty six three 10-7), proven in Equation 2 (Harris, 2010). Because carbonic acid is a polyprotic acid dissociating more than one steps, an in-intensity know-how of CO_2 dissolution calls for that the second one acid dissociation step, i.e.,

$HCO3^{-}$ (aq) ------------- $CO3^{2-}$(aq) + H^{+}

The electrochemical reactions are composed of anodic response of sodium steel oxidation (Equation three) and cathodic response of hydrogen evolution (Equation 4):

Anodic reaction: 2Na ------------- $2Na^+ + 2e$ $E^o = -2.71$ V (Equation 3)

Cathodic reaction: $2H^+ + 2e$ ------------- $H_2(g)$ $E^o = 0.00$ V (Equation 4)

Net equation: $2Na + 2H^+$ ------------- $2Na^+ + H_2(g)$ $E^o = 2.71$ V (Equation 5)

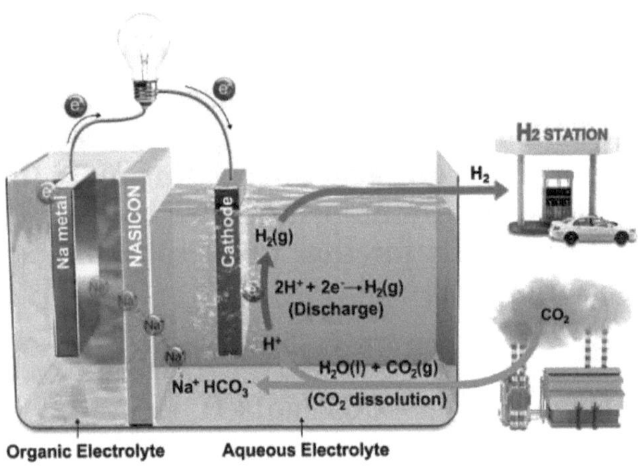

Working diagram

Then, the electrochemical internet equation is certainly given because the oxidation of Na

metallic and the spontaneous evolution of hydrogen (Equation 5). Because the capacity of cathodic response is carefully motivated through the pH of aqueous solution, the dissolution of CO_2 renders a good electrochemical response environment through acidifying the aqueous solution.

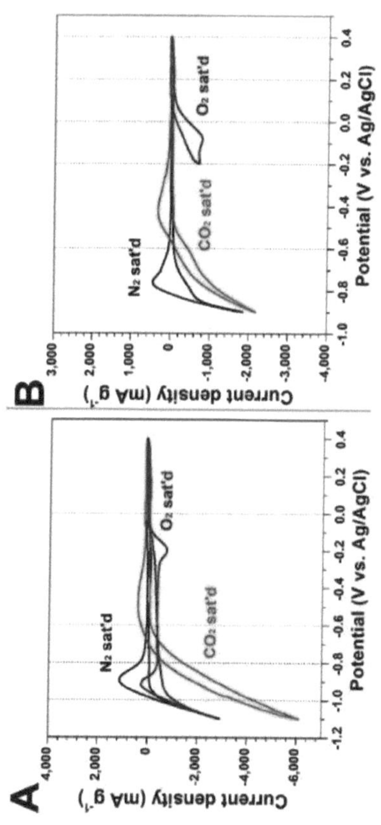

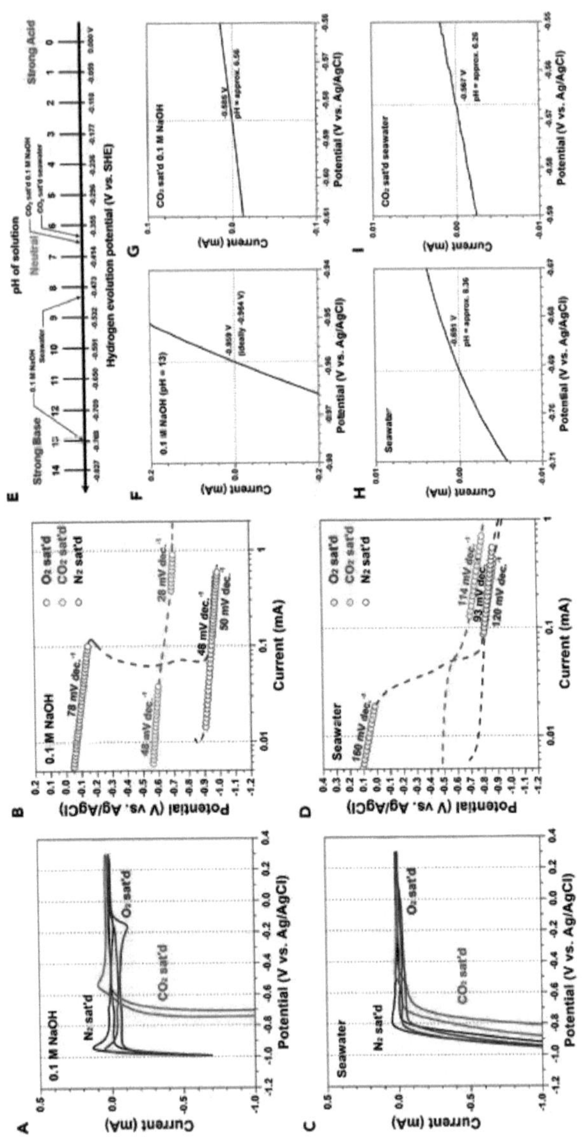
A
0.1 M NaOH
N2 sat'd
CO2 sat'd
O2 sat'd
Current (mA)
Potential (V vs. Ag/AgCl)
B
0.1 M NaOH
O2 sat'd
CO2 sat'd
N2 sat'd
78 mV dec.-1
48 mV dec.-1
28 mV dec.-1
50 mV dec.-1
Potential (V vs. Ag/AgCl)
Current (mA)
C
Seawater
N2 sat'd
CO2 sat'd
O2 sat'd
Current (mA)
Potential (V vs. Ag/AgCl)
D
Seawater
O2 sat'd
CO2 sat'd
N2 sat'd
160 mV dec.-1
114 mV dec.-1
93 mV dec.-1
120 mV dec.-1
Potential (V vs. Ag/AgCl)
Current (mA)
E
pH of solution
Strong Base
Neutral
Strong Acid
0.1 M NaOH
Seawater
Hydrogen evolution potential (V vs. SHE)
F
0.1 M NaOH (pH = 13)
Current (mA)
Potential (V vs. Ag/AgCl)
G
CO2 sat'd 0.1 M NaOH
Current (mA)
Potential (V vs. Ag/AgCl)
H
Seawater
Current (mA)
Potential (V vs. Ag/AgCl)
I
CO2 sat'd seawater
Current (mA)
Potential (V vs. Ag/AgCl)

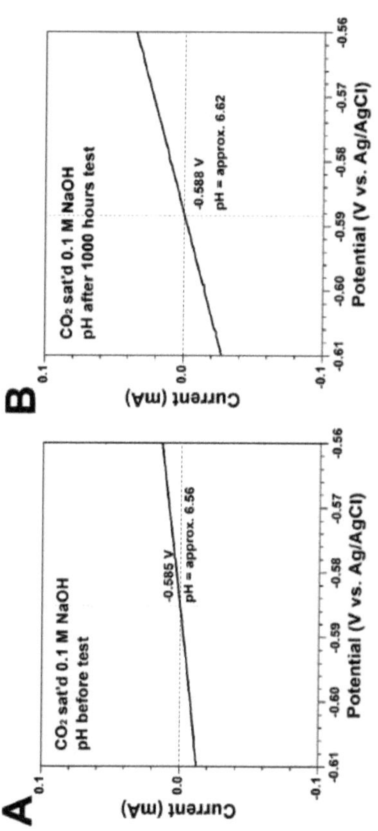
A
CO₂ sat'd 0.1 M NaOH
pH before test
-0.585 V
pH = approx. 6.56
Current (mA)
0.1
0.0
-0.1
-0.61
-0.60
-0.59
-0.58
-0.57
-0.56
Potential (V vs. Ag/AgCl)
B
CO₂ sat'd 0.1 M NaOH
pH after 1000 hours test
-0.588 V
pH = approx. 6.62
Current (mA)
0.1
0.0
-0.1
-0.61
-0.60
-0.59
-0.58
-0.57
-0.56
Potential (V vs. Ag/AgCl)

TWENTY-FOUR

RESULT

Therefore, in this way, by replacing coal in power generation, the advantage of acetylene gas is that there is not much gas mixture in the exhaust that comes out in it, so we can use those gases also. We also make acetylene gas through calcium carbide, and purified water. In this process we get biproduct calcium hydroxide, for which the market doors are open.

Therefore, through this type of power plant, we can not only generate power but also save our environment from harmful gases. And if the products generated by the power plant like calcium hydroxide and electricity and Hydrogen gas are properly transported to the right market, then we will find this multipurpose power plant more economical than the old power plant.

TWENTY-FIVE
CONCLUSION

Eventually we saw that we obtained energy from acetylene gas to convert boiler water into steam, and we also obtained acetylene gas from the chemical reaction of calcium carbide and water; after that a biproduct calcium hydroxide, was formed in this process.

After burning acetylene, we did not directly throw its exhaust into the environment, after removing the pure carbon dioxide from it, sent it to the electrochemical cell for chemical process; here after chemical reactions, our exhaust was converted into hydrogen gas and electricity and this formed hydrogen We can use the gas again as fuel. In this way we have also used the exhaust and saw the proposal of such a power plant which will be more efficient than before and will not harm the environment.

TWENTY-SIX
REFERENCES

1. Dalton's Law of Partial Pressures curated by Ed Vitz, John W. Moore, Justin Shorb, Xavier Prat-Resina, Tim Wendorff, & Adam Hahn.
2. NIST Chemistry WebBook OECD/IEA Electricity Information (various editions) International Gas Union, Natural Gas Conversion Guide
3. Kim, Changmin & Kim, Jeongwon & Joo, Sangwook & Bu, Yunfei & Liu, Meilin & Cho, Jaephil & Kim, Guntae. (2018). Efficient CO2 Utilization via a Hybrid Na-CO2 System Based on CO2 Dissolution. iScience. 9. 10.1016/j.isci.2018.10.027.
4. 8 REFERENCES Ahn, W., Park, M.G., Lee, D.U., Seo, M.H., Jiang, G., Cano, Z.P., Hassan, F.M., and Chen, Z. (2018). Hollow multivoid nanocuboids derived from ternary Ni-Co-Fe prussian blue analog for dualelectrolysis of oxygen and hydrogen evolution reactions. Adv. Funct. Mater. 28, 1802129..
5. Akgerman, C. E.; Ghoreishi, S.M. (1992). Supercritical extraction of hexachlorobenzene from soil, Ind. Eng. Chem. Res., Vol.31, No.1, pp.333–339 Armor, J.N. (2000).

6. Catalytic fixation of CO_2, CO_2 purity, energy, and the environment, Am. Chem. Soc. Div. Petrol. Chem. Prepr., Vol.45, No.1, pp.141–142 Audus, H.; Kaarstad O. & Kowal M. (1996). Decarbonisation of fossil fuels: hydrogen as an energy carrier.
7. Proc 11th World Hydrogen Energy Conference, Int. Assoc. of Hydrogen Energy, published by Schon and Wetzel, Frankfurt, Germany Ayers, W. M. (Ed.) (1988).
8. Catalytic Activation of Carbon Dioxide; ACS Symposium Series 363; American Chemical Society: New York Climate Change: Forests and Carbon Sequestration (2007). Temperate Forest Foundation Vol.16, No.2
9. Singh Patel, Gaurav. (2022). Dry Ice Acetylene Power Plant (Dia Power Plant). 10.22214/ijraset.2022.41969.
10. Al Sadat, W.I., and Archer, L.A. (2016). The O_2- assisted Al/CO_2 electrochemical cell: a system for CO_2 capture/ conversion and electric power generation. Sci. Adv. 2, e1600968. Andersen, S.O. (2017). We can and must govern climate engineering. Nature 551, 415. Angamuthu, R., Byers, P., Lutz, M., Spek, A.L., and Bouwman, E. (2010). Electrocatalytic CO_2 conversion to oxalate by a copper complex. Science 327, 313–315.
11. Bourzac, K. (2017). We have the technology. Nature 550, S66–S69. Bu, Y., Gwon, O., Nam, G., Jang, H., Kim, S., Zhong, Q., Cho, J., and Kim, G. (2017). A highly efficient and robust cation ordered perovskite oxide as a bifunctional catalyst for rechargeable Zinc-air batteries. ACS Nano 11, 11594–11601.
12. Torp, T. & Gale, J. (2002). Demonstrating storage of CO_2 in geological reservoirs: the Sleipner and Sacs projects, 6th International Conference on Greenhouse Gas Control Technologies (GHGT-6), Kyoto, Japan, Oct.2002, Elsevier Science Ltd, Oxford,

13. UK UNFCCC, The Kyoto Protocol to the UN Framework Convention on Climate Change (UNFCCC-1992)
14. WRI, (2008). CCS Guidelines: Guidelines for Carbon Dioxide Capture, Transport, and Storage. Washington, DC: WRI. Published by World Resources Institute
15. Darensbourg, D.J. (2007). Making plastics from carbon dioxide: salen metal complexes as catalysts for the production of polycarbonates from epoxides and CO2. Chem. Rev. 107, 2388–2410.
16. Das, S.K., Xu, S., and Archer, L.A. (2013). Carbon dioxide assist for non-aqueous sodium-oxygen batteries. Electrochem. Commun. 27, 59–62.
17. Stewart C. & Hessami M. (2005). A study of methods of carbon dioxide capture and sequestration–the Sustainability of a photosynthetic bioreactor approach, Energy Conversion and Management, 46: 403–420
18. Stolaroff J K, Lowry G V, Keith D W, (2005). Using CaO- and MgO-rich industrial waste streams for carbon sequestration. Energy Conversion and Management, 46: 687–699
19. Dowell, N.M., Fennell, P.S., Shah, N., and Maitland, G.C. (2017). The role of CO2 capture and utilization in mitigating climate change. Nat. Clim. Chang. 7, 243–249.
20. Harris, D.C. (2010).Quantitative ChemicalAnalysis, Eight edition (W. H. Freeman and Company).

9 798887 044040

Printed by Libri Plureos GmbH in Hamburg, Germany